THE STAR OF DESTINY
and
THE GERMAN'S TALE

By John Galt

Edited and Introduction by David J. Knight

Foreword by Ian McGhee

Vocamus Editions
Guelph, Ontario

The Star of Destiny was first published in John Galt's *Autobiography* by Cochrane and McCrone in 1833. *The German's Tale* was first published in *Rothelan: A Romance of the English Histories* by Oliver & Boyd in 1824.

Edited and Introduction by David J. Knight

Foreword by Ian McGhee

Cover image by Sona Mincoff

Cover design by Liz Morant

ISBN 13: 978-1-928171-15-7 (pbk)
ISBN 13: 978-1-928171-16-4 (ebk)

Vocamus Editions
130 Dublin Street, North
Guelph, Ontario, Canada
N1H 4N4

www.vocamus.net

2015

In Memory of
Sue Richards (February 9, 1958 – August 2, 2014)

TABLE OF CONTENTS

ACKNOWLEDGEMENTS

I would like to thank my parents and the generosity of those who have made this book possible, especially Jeremy Luke Hill of Vocamus Press. I would also like to thank Liz Morant for the cover design, Sona Mincoff for the cover oil painting *Intransigent* (2013), and Ian McGhee of The John Galt Society (Ayrshire) for writing the Foreword. Thank you also to Lynn Broughton, and to Scott McGovern for his enthusiastic encouragement.

FOREWORD

by Ian McGhee

This is a good time to become involved with John Galt. For too long he has unjustly been neglected, but there are signs that this is being rectified. At the 2014 World Congress of Scottish Literatures there were no less than three discussion panels devoted to aspects of Galt's literary output. Within the last three years there have been published a collection of essays on his work by a formidable list of eminent scholars[1] and Publication Studio Guelph has published a new edition of *The Omen*. Most encouraging of all, a John Galt Society has just been formed to encourage the study and appreciation of his life and work.

So why all this interest in a man who was born in Irvine, Scotland in 1789 and died in Greenock in 1839? In his native country Galt is mainly remembered as an author who anatomized small town life around the turn of the nineteenth century. In novels such as *The Annals of the Parish* or *The Provost*, which he called "theoretical histories" or which we might nowadays term dramatized documentaries, he skil-

---

[1] i.e. Hewitt 2012.

FOREWORD

fully and ironically pointed up the social, religious and economic changes which the Industrial Revolution was bringing. In Canada, the land in which he invested so much of his hopes and in which he maintained a steadfast belief of eventual greatness, his chief legacy is as a founder of cities and builder of communities.

Galt was aware of his worth as an author, and often relied on his pen for an income, but despite the money and celebrity which writing brought, it never wholly satisfied him. In his novel *Bogle Corbet* he has the eponymous hero say, "The fates preserve me from ever having anything to do with such a trade [writing books]," and add that "only the secondary and inferior of mankind make it a profession; no great man ever only wrote books."[2] In one of his autobiographies Galt himself says, "I have ever held literature to be a secondary pursuit,"[3] and in the other, "I have sometimes felt a little shame-faced in thinking myself so much an author... A mere literary man – an author by profession – stands but low in my opinion."[4]

Business was the arena in which he hoped to make his mark and his fortune. Unfortunately his business career was marked by bad luck, bad timing and, it has to be admit-

---

[2] Galt, *Bogle Corbet: or The Emigrants*, London, Colburn and Bentley, 1830, Vol II, p 139.

[3] Galt, *My Literary Life and Miscellanies*, Edinburgh, William Blackwood, 1834, Vol. I, p 313.

[4] Galt, *The Autobiography*, London, Cochrane and McCrone, 1833, p 200.

ted, bad decisions. He left Scotland in 1804 and, bankrolled by his father, entered into a partnership with Hugh McLachlan in 1807, but their company went bankrupt in 1809. The experience was not wholly wasted since it provides the basis for a significant episode in *Bogle Corbet* where the hero's business fails because of the shortcomings of his partner. Galt had one great success when he acted as Parliamentary Agent for the Union Canal Company. His lobbying and "fixing" of the Parliamentarians ensured the passage of the necessary legislation and led to him becoming involved with Canada as the agent, appointed on a no win – no fee basis, to secure compensation for losses suffered by some Canadians in the War of 1812.

That ultimately proved unsuccessful, but it did lead to the formation of the Canada Company and Galt's period in Canada. His work there laid the basis for the Company's business model for the next few decades, and his community-building policies were amply vindicated. At the time, however, he fell foul of both the Provincial Government and his Directors in London. He was recalled, relieved of his position and even had to endure a spell in debtors' prison.

Over all his life, on crests or in troughs, Galt wrote, and there was no genre to which he did not apply his pen. Magazine articles on politics, economics and society, histories, biographies, travel books, short stories, novels, children's text books, poems and plays were all published under a variety of pseudonyms and with varying degrees of success.

FOREWORD

Galt's personal beliefs were consistent, but he behaved to others on the basis of what he observed rather than dogmatic principle. Throughout his life he adhered to the Presbyterian faith of his childhood and has his characters such as Dr. Pringle in *The Ayrshire Legatees* and Lawrie Todd in the novel of the same name assert and uphold the rights of the Church of Scotland. Yet when he laid out the town plan of Guelph he reserved prime sites for Episcopalian and Catholic as well as Presbyterian churches and recommended to his Directors that all three should be gifted to the respective denominations. He tended to be dismissive of sectarian certitudes.

His attitude to politics was similar. Despite claiming that he had never "been a politician all my life"[5] he certainly knew how politics worked as can be seen in the detailed descriptions in *The Provost*, *The Member* and *The Radical*, his trio of novels devoted to that topic. He himself was "always a moderate Tory," saying, "I have never been able to discern that there was aught in political persuasion, different from my own, to justify enmity."[6] He tells us, "I was surely born a Radical, and owe my Tory predilections entirely to a prankful elf, who, delighting in the ridiculous... ever turned towards me the comic aspect of things."[7] In politics as in re-

---

[5] *The Autobiography*, II, p 7.
[6] *The Autobiography*, II, p 229.
[7] *My Literary Life and Miscellanies*, I, p 235.

FOREWORD

ligion Galt was an empiricist and judged people by actions and outcomes rather than fixed beliefs.

Despite this rational approach to everyday life Galt had a part of him that wondered about the supernatural and the uncanny. Though the rational product of the Enlightenment, he spent his childhood listening to stories told by the old women who lived near his grandmother in Irvine. As with all folk tales these stories had ghosts and magic and happenings beyond the ken of human understanding. Galt certainly incorporated such elements in some of his fictions like the novel *The Spaewife* (a spaewife is a sorceress) and short stories like "The Spectre Ship of Salem".

The central motif of *The Star of Destiny* is not therefore an aberration but chimes with Galt's fascination with the occult. Furthermore, the notion that a star determines the actions of a man throughout his life is not a great conceptual leap from Galt's belief, orthodox for the Calvinism of his time, in predestination. This play and related short story are not among the best-known of Galt's works, but they do highlight an important part of his mental make-up. More than that they exist to be enjoyed and Vocamus Editions is to be commended for publishing an edition which allows us to do just that.

IAN McGHEE
Secretary, John Galt Society
Ayrshire, Scotland
2015

xv

FOREWORD

References

Hewitt, Regina. John Galt: Observations and Conjectures on Literature, History, and Society. *Transits: Literature, Thought & Culture, 1650–1850.* New York: Lexington Books, 2012.

Galt, John. *My Literary Life and Miscellanies,* Edinburgh; William Blackwood, 1834.

Galt, John. *The Autobiography,* London, Cochrane and Mc-Crone, 1833.

Galt, John. *Bogle Corbet: or The Emigrants,* London; Colburn and Bentley, 1830.

INTRODUCTION

by David J. Knight

John Galt's "peculiar dramatic essay" *The Star of Destiny* is a verse drama written c.1818 that draws on the Gothic tradition of books like Lord Byron's *Manfred* and Goethe's *Faust*. It is accompanied in this volume by *The German's Tale*, Galt's 1824 prose reworking of the story, which he included in his 1833 *Autobiography*. Both versions of the story revolve around Herman, a scholar who trades his soul for supernatural knowledge and earthly advantage, a figure common to the German Gothic.

The influence of Lord Byron and his literary circle on *The Star of Destiny* is pronounced. Galt noted in his 1833 *Autobiography*[1] that *The Star of Destiny* was written shortly after Byron's *Manfred* (1816–1817) and was intended to be "a more scenic version" of that text. He also mentions that *The German's Tale* "draws on Goethe's *Faust* via Byron's *Manfred*."[2] As I have suggested elsewhere,[3] Galt was deeply

---

[1] See Galt's Preface below.

[2] Hewitt 2012:335.

[3] In my Foreword to *The Omen by John Galt* (Guelph: Publication Studio, 2013).

INTRODUCTION

affected by Byron and the writings of the poet's extended literary circle, namely Percy Bysshe and Mary Shelley (*née* Wollstonecraft Godwin). In light of these influences, it is interesting that Mary Shelley's *Frankenstein: or, The Modern Prometheus* also appeared, albeit anonymously, in 1818, when Galt was writing *Destiny*. It is also noteworthy that Galt reworked *The Star of Destiny* into prose form, as *The German's Tale*, the same year his friend Lord Byron died (1824), and therefore the story is not only Galt's bow of recognition to that poet's contribution in its inception, but also a commemoration and prosaic epitaph that may be seen as an accompaniment to Galt's later *Life of Byron* (1830).

The Germanic Gothic atmosphere of *Faust, Manfred* and *Frankenstein* can be sensed throughout *The Star of Destiny*. The story is Faustian in that the protagonist Herman becomes entwined with a demonic familiar. Herman's alchemical experiments and his acquisition of an ancient Kabalistic grimoire, together with the fairytale-like Bavarian setting and historical personages of the 13th century Royal House of Welf (Guelph), clothe both the play and tale with the stylistic elements of Gothic romance and directly conduct the zeitgeist of early horror fiction. In so doing, Galt was effectively mythologizing the historical Germanic context of the British royal family. It is with these deeper meanings that Galt probably decided in 1827 to name his new city, in the Upper Canada wilderness, Guelph.

John Galt's choice of character names often directly references these Gothic works and other texts in the epic tradition. The name Herman, for instance, is that of a servant in Byron's *Manfred*, a Faustian poetic drama set in the Alps. The name Gondibert is from both Duke Gondibert, a historical figure of the Lombardic royal line, and from *Gondibert*, an unfinished "heroick" epic poem by Sir William Davenant (1606–1668).[4] The name Beatrice appears as one of Dante's guides in the last book of the *Divine Comedy*, *Paradiso*, and in the last four *canti* of *Purgatorio*.[5] These names all clearly indicate the literary tradition in which Galt is situating his story.

Others names serve to reference *The Star of Destiny*'s medieval Germanic setting. For example, Emperor Henry, the Birder may be Galt's version of Henry the Lion (1129–1195), a member of the Welf dynasty.[6] The name Herman also appears historically as Herman V, who ruled Verona and Baden from 1190 and founded the cities of Backnang, Pforzheim, and Stuttgart. These historical connections serve to place *The Star of Destiny* and *The German's Tale* firmly within the medieval Germanic ouevre.

---

[4] *Gondibert* is set in late antique Italy, when the Lombards were victorious against the Vandals. It was printed in 1651 by John Holden, London.

[5] Beatrice has been commonly identified as the Florentine woman Beatrice "Bice" di Folco Portinari (1266–1290).

[6] He was Duke of Saxony, as Henry III, from 1142, and Duke of Bavaria, as Henry XII, from 1156, which duchies he held until 1180, when he was ousted by the rival Hohenstaufen dynasty.

INTRODUCTION

Galt's deliberate use of antiquated words also contributes to this atmosphere. Galt's choice of words such as *chymicks* and *chace*, no longer in common usage in the early 19th century, are intentionally re-used in his play to give it the weight of historicity. *Mangaul* is one such obsolete word, described later as a cauldron, or a "chymic pot, being with calx surcharged" (Ventrose in Act I, scene II), where *Chymic* is a chemical and *Calx* is a residual substance that remains when a metal or mineral combusts or becomes calcinated due to heat. These kinds of archaisms help situate the story in an ancient period, and because they are all associated with alchemy, they also heighten the story's mysticism.

The central image of Galt's tale, the natal star, or the star of destiny, reinforces this supernatural setting and also connects it firmly to the idea of predestination, which was of great interest to him during the mid–1820s, as can also be seen in his novel, *The Omen* (1825). Galt takes the idea of the natal star from a near east tradition that would have been available to him through works like John Selden's *Syrian Deities*,[7] which is referenced in this passage from *The Gentleman's Magazine, and Historical Chronicle*:

> According to the tenets of the ancient Chaldean and Egyptian astrology, the cause of all the causes in this lower world depended on the stars, and must be referred to them, they made fortune depend on the moon; and the

---

[7]John Selden, *De diis Syriis* or *Syrian Deities*, 1617.

INTRODUCTION

daemon, that is to say, the genius, on the sun. This genius is that which presides at the birth of men.[8]

The natal star is thus both resonant with the arcane mystery of the near east and connected to an idea of fate and destiny parallel to the Calvinist predestination that so interested Galt during this period. The conflict between these two elements is central to the tension that drives the story of *The Star of Destiny* and the central character of Herman.

Considering the antique setting, the supernatural atmosphere, and the role of fate or predestination, it is interesting that Galt intended *The Star of Destiny* to be performed via a mechanistic theatrical manipulation known as the Eidophusikon, one of the modern wonders of the period. The Eidophusikon was a piece of art and mechanical theatre created by Philip James de Loutherbourg (1740–1812).[9] This device was described by the media of the day as "Moving Pictures, representing Phenomena of Nature," and can now be considered an early form of film making. The effect was achieved by paintings, mirrors and pulleys. Loutherbourg first exhibited this in Leicester Square, London, in February

---

[8] E. Cave, *The Gentleman's Magazine, and Historical Chronicle* Volume 41 (1771): Pp.10–11.

[9] Also known as Jacques–Philippe de Loutherbourg, he was an English painter of French origin who was David Garrick's scenery designer.

INTRODUCTION

of 1781, and Galt's intended usage of it places him at the forefront of early developments in moving media history.[10]

It is therefore altogether appropriate that Galt's *The Star of Destiny* and *The German's Tale*, drawing on past traditions while at the same time intended to be shown through modern means, should now represent a tradition of Guelph writing, theatre and audio–visual multi–media arts being reissued to a contemporary audience.

DAVID J. KNIGHT
General Editor – Vocamus Editions
Guelph, Ontario, Canada
2015

---

[10]This aspect of Galt's creative output has not yet been seriously explored, though I briefly mentioned this in my Foreword to *The Omen* (see above note 10).

INTRODUCTION

Further Reading

Cave, E. (ed.). *The Gentleman's Magazine, and Historical Chronicle*; Volume 41, 1771.

Knight, David J. (ed.). *The Omen by John Galt.* Guelph: Publication Studio Guelph, 2013.

Waterston, Elizabeth. John Galt and the Canadian Star of Destiny. *Canadian Literature* 129. Pp. 116-127. Vancouver: University of British Columbia, 1991.

Waterston, Elizabeth (ed.). *John Galt: Reappraisals.* Guelph: University of Guelph, 1985.

PREFACE

by John Galt

The selection of materials for my *Autobiography*,[1] has not proved voluminous; and therefore, to give the reader his full pennyworth, I have ventured to subjoin an unpublished peculiar dramatic essay. It was written many years ago, soon after *Manfred* appeared,[2] and was intended to present a more scenic version of the same kind of subject. It seemed to me, that the sublimity of Byron's beautiful drama, was too refined and meditative for representation, and this notion emboldened me to fuse the mystery of Faustus again, and to mix it with baser stuff, for the use of the million, as gold is alloyed for purposes of circulation. This is all I can say, in excuse for the faults of the scenes intended to vary the tenour of the piece: the serious defects are a more inveterate and fatal inheritance.

In adapting the story for exhibition, it was necessary to conceal the allegory, but not so entirely as that it should not

---

[1]John Galt 1833. *The Autobiography of John Galt.* Cochrane and M'Crone.

[2]By Byron 1816–1817.

be obvious. Still, however, it is done, perhaps, so effectually, that many readers may require to be told Count Herman is really only a crazy lover, and that all the silent servitude of the fiend, is but the phantasy of his morbid and moody imaginations.

It ought to be mentioned here, what, indeed, will require no interpreter to explain, – namely, that the subjoined sketch neither belongs to the legitimate drama, nor to melodramatic composition. It was imagined, that the large theatres were not very well calculated for the representation of regular plays, and that, possibly, in the present dearth and scarcity of them, some sort of exhibition might be rendered popular, which should combine intellectual energy with visible magnificence. The subsequent essay is an attempt to construct a work of this kind. I have endeavoured to introduce a dialogue that may be heard, and a series of exhibitions that may be viewed, which shall be more impressive than pantomime, and equally gorgeous in the spectacle.

Some time ago, before my last illness, while meditating on this conception, I intended to draw the attention of Mr. Stanfield[3] to the subject, and actually appointed a meeting with him, to explain my idea, when prevented by indisposition. My project was, to introduce upon the stage something equivalent to books of travel. For example, to explain to him that a very splendid and rational exhibition might be produced, by representing, as I proposed to do, for a first

---

[3] Clarkson Frederick Stanfield (1793–1867).

pageant, a traveller ascending the Nile, giving, in the course of the voyage, all the striking views of Egypt on the one side, and in the return, to perform the same thing for those on the other.

This was intended as the substratum of the piece; a fable, however, might be engrafted on it; but that was not so essential, as to make the audience see all the choice things which would appear to the traveller, and receive such an oral description as would make the exhibition approximate to the truth and instruction of traveling.

My reason for fixing on the Nile for the first of the series, was, because I thought it furnished the best materials for scenic pomp; but my idea was, to embrace all interesting tours, and instead of acting plays, to adapt travels to representation. Ill health has prevented me from following out the idea, but a splendid, instructive, and most interesting amusement might be formed on this basis.

Nor did my fancy stop here: it seemed to me, that histories and novels might be also represented, and that now, when dramas with dialogue could no longer be acted with success, a species of dumb show might be exhibited, that would not be inexplicable; but I can only throw out the notion for others to work with. Othello's occupation is literally gone, and something else must be tried.

Combined with scenery, well painted, and correct in circumstances, I would have, now and then, living pictures introduced, in which accomplished actors, especially posture-masters, could perform, and suitable musical accompani-

PREFACE

ments made to enhance the illusion, and increase the delight of the scene.

Though not exactly a work falling under the class which I conceive might be thus fitted for representation, the *Star of Destiny* gave rise to the idea, and it is for those of more skill, health, and leisure, to consider, by observing the construction of it, with this explanation, how far, in the existing state of theatrical pageants, the plan is worthy of being tried.

JOHN GALT
31st August,1833

THE STAR OF DESTINY

and

THE GERMAN'S TALE

By John Galt

THE STAR OF DESTINY

Dramatis Personae

Men
EMPEROR HENRY
HERMAN
VENTOSE
1st CITIZEN
2nd CITIZEN
SIR GONDIBERT
BOY
LUDOLPH
RUGENSTEIN
LUNENBURGH
SERVANT
BENEDICT
BERNSTEIN
PRIOR
INQUISITOR

Women
1st WOMAN
2nd WOMAN
BEATRICE
MERL

Chorus
Men
Women
Huntsmen

Mutes, Fiend, Child, Servants, Inquisitors, Courtiers and Attendants

ACT I

Scene I – A Gothic Study

[*Window opens – shews a beautiful Star, whose radiance appears occasionally to fade and expand. In the middle of the room a magical mangaul burning. –* HERMAN, *seated at a table, with an antique volume in his hand; a dagger and a lamp on the table.*]

HERMAN: O'er every birth a star of fate presides,
And he that knows his orb of destiny,
May, by the changes of its radiance, tell
Whene'er his good or evil genius reigns.
This knowledge, earned by many a midnight vigil,
Has taught me that yon silver star is mine,
Which nightly, since I conn'd this wond'rous volume,
Hath dimm'd its fires, and warn'd me to forbear.
Yet have I still undaunted read, and now,
10 While pale and fitfully its beams shrink in,
The ingredients of a potent spell I mingle,
And but three drops of my own blood are wanting,
To give me proof that to my hests and bidding,
A spirit of dread ministry will come.

THE STAR OF DESTINY

[*Rises.*] Why should the glorious planet fade at this?
Is there then peril to my better part
In this mysterious science? If I stop,
Haw shall I know the secrets written here
Are knowledge or phantasma? Can there be
Evil in truth? For to unfold the art
That summons spirits from their dark abode,
Is but to know what is – and what the gods,
In their eternal mysteries have framed. –
Shrink into darkness thou faint trembling light,
I will abide the issues of the spell.

[*He lays down the book, and taking the dagger, holding his arm over the cauldron, pierces a vein.*]

The blood refuses. Why will it not come?
It was no groan! 'Tis but the sighing wind,
That sweeps along the silent galleries.
What coward palsy am I smitten with?
I'll strike again. It flows – so now 'tis done.

[*Subterranean noises heard, and a large gaunt hand holding a scroll rises from the middle of the cauldron.*]

What a horrible apocalypse is this?

[*He takes the scroll and reads.*]

7

THE STAR OF DESTINY

'If thou on All Soul's Eve wilt be but mine,
To all thy wishes I will be thy slave.' –
Who and what art thou? Show me first thy face, –
The strong condition of thy proffer'd service.[1]

[*The scroll vanishes from his hand, solemn music is heard, and
a flood of light bursts in from the side scene.*]

Hail, thou magnificent refulgent form,
I would not seek to serve a brighter god.
Show me thy power, and what I may expect.

[*The light disappears, and a procession of slaves, bearing trea-
sure, is seen to pass in the air, outside of the window.*]

40
He can give wealth, – treasures would beggar kings –
And I may purchase all that gold can buy;
But love or friendship cannot be so won,
And what is life without them? Pass away,
I will not stoop to take the sordid trash!

[*The vision changes, martial music is heard, an army is seen
defiling among mountains, and venerable men come from the
gate of a gorgeous city, bearing a crown and sceptre.*]

What means this glorious pageantry of war,
And these hoar senators, who thus come forth,

---

[1]See *The German's Tale* for the alternative text.

THE STAR OF DESTINY

Bearing the emblems of imperial state?
They point towards yon myriads of the brave,
That throng the hills, like the bright seraphim
Reposing on the golden evening clouds: –
And now they kneel and offer me the crown.
Ha! would he bribe me with ambition's bauble,
And place me on a far–seen pinnacle,
An idol in the sunshine, to be cast
Into a darker and a deeper ruin
Than gulfs the common fortunes of mankind?
Vanish, ye hollow and fantastic pomps!
I have not studied to be fooled by shows.

[*The vision changes, and* SIR GONDIBERT *is seen in a wild and desolate place, with his hands bound: – troubled and mournful music heard.*]

My rival Gondibert. – Canst thou give him, –
Surrender him, to my awaken'd hate?
No, Spirit, no; I'll not be brib'd by this.
His noble nature won fair Beatrice,
And though I mourn that lovely maid's denial,
I bear no malice to her gallant choice.
Away, brave Gondibert, live for thy love!

[*The vision changes, and* BEATRICE *is seen reposing in a splendid apartment – delightful soft music.*]

Wilt thou give Beatrice? O let me catch her;

On this condition I am thine for ever.

[*The vision vanishes; the stage is darkened, and a wavering form of the demon is seen, amidst thunder and lightning, exulting over* HERMAN.]

Oh, horror, horror! Hell! must I be thine?

[*Exit* HERMAN; *dreadful thunder and lightning.*]

Scene II – A Street.

[*An ancient College seen on fire at a distance – bells ringing – a crowd of people rushing from all quarters, and in such garbs as may be supposed hastily put on in a moment of alarm.*]

CHORUS: Mercy on us! What's the matter?
Stop your clamour – cease your clatter.
'Tis a fire; fire, fire;
Where, where?
There, there,
See it burns,
In the air;
Higher, higher, higher, higher.
Oh, the flames, how they mount!
How they wrestle, lick, and point –
The students and the college,
The professors and their knowledge;

THE STAR OF DESTINY

Their cellars and their libraries,
Their wigs, and gowns, and pageantries;
Their mutton, beef, and bacon,
Their turkeys, geese, and capon;
Their physics, rhyme, and reason,
And their delicates in season,
All, all, but serve as fuel,
To the flames so fierce and cruel.
See, how they clasp the steeple;
It shakes – it will come down;
Lord have mercy on the people,
It will murder half the town!

[The steeple falls with a great crash, the flames are extinguished, and the bell ceases to ring.]

[Enter VENTOSE, with a petticoat on, and a large powdered wig.]

VENTOSE: Obstreperous nightingales! home to your
nests;
Nor with nocturnal clamour deafen thus
The solemn night, that is already dumb.

1st WOMAN: How has this happened?

2nd WOMAN: Tell us, tell us, do.

VENTOSE: Peace, matron, peace. Art not ashamed,
30   old hag,
Thus in the street, and at the midnight hour,
To shew thyself with breeches for a shawl?

2nd WOMAN: And fellow, where got you this
      petticoat?

VENTOSE: A fig-leaf in the hurry pluck'd.

1st CITIZEN: And this? –

2nd CITIZEN: It is the rector's wig! how came it here?

VENTOSE: The hand of instinct placed it on my head.

1st WOMAN: But tell us, tell us how the fire began –
      What lives lost –
who perished in the flames?

VENTOSE: Save those whose burglaries and petty
40   thefts
Vex the sweet temper of good housewifes, none,
None perished in the flames.

2nd WOMAN: What does he mean?

VENTOSE: The vulgar jargon calls them rats and
      mice.

THE STAR OF DESTINY

As for the fire, wherein they were consum'd,
And now in ashes pale infect the air,
That 'gan in the renowned Count Herman's chamber;
Whose chymic pot, being with calx surcharged,
Of most combustible and testy humour,
Crack'd, and went off in those ambitious fires,
Which you have seen flapping the cheeks of Heaven.

1st CITIZEN: And has the Count himself escaped
        unhurt?

VENTOSE: In lith and limb, member and joint, he has;
But what infection from the fume he took
Into his nostrils, making sick the brain,
Cannot be told; but like a thing distraught,
He rous'd the college with his scalded yells.
I started at the sound; and oh, sad vision!
Beheld him in the court – his stockings down,
And not a coat upon his helpless back,
Unslipper'd, pacing wild; while all on fire,
The riven rafters of his chamber roof,
Did burn like Erebus, or town of Try,
What time Minerva, and the goddess proud,
Turn'd old queen Hecuba into a bitch,
That gnaw'd the heel of many a Greek that night.
But ladies now, and courteous gentlemen,
Let's all repair unto our several homes,
And doff these garbs, wherein we dressed ourselves

70   In such confounded hurry. For this fire,
Longer to stay were to incur a cold,
Or deadly cough; therefore to bed, to bed.

[*Exeunt severally.*]

Scene III – A Glade in a Wood

[*Enter* SIR GONDIBERT, BEATRICE, MERL, *children and attendants.*]

SIR GONDIBERT: It is a lovely sylvan solitude.
Here the meek primrose earliest lifts her eye;
The daisy here, on the smooth grassy knoll,
Smirks a bright welcome to the vernal sun;
While yet the spring has scarcely dared to pass
From midst the branches of the neighbouring grove.

BEATRICE: The mavis and the linnet mingle songs
With the bold blackbird's full, round note of joy.
The solemn jays here chatter garrulous,
10   Like blithsome gossips in a nappy nook;
And choughs and rooks forget their boding here,
To caw repose. The humming waterfall
Sings like a nurse, a soothing lullaby.

BOY: How tame the butterflies are in this place.
Three have I caught; look, bright as the pea blossom;

14

THE STAR OF DESTINY

And I have chased a golden honey bee
From flower to flower, till I can run no longer.

BEATRICE: Then sit thee down, sweet rogue, and rest
        thyself;
And Merl, till the village dancers come,
Invoke the wood-nymphs to our revelry.

[SIR GONDIBERT, *BEATRICE, and children sit.*]

MERL [*sings*].

Ode to the Wood–Nymphs.

Come, ye nymphs, whose eyes like dew,
Twinkle these green branches through;
Whose timid steps are only heard,
When rustling wind, or hopping bird,
Stirs the fallen leaves so sear,
Come ye wood–nymphs softly here –
Softly come, and with you bring,
Flowers and fragrancies of spring;
With the ripen'd apples' blushes,
Peeping forth the bowery bushes:
Bashful whisp'ring they appear –
Come ye gentle wood–nymphs here.
Hasten, for the summer gales,
Slumber in the new mown vales,
And bring with you leafy boughs,

15

To fan our dancers' glowing brows;
Garlands too, for maids to wear,
40   Bring, sweet nymphs: – Our pastimes share.

[SIR GONDIBERT *and* BEATRICE *come forward* – HERMAN *is seen at a distance.*]

SIR GONDIBERT: It is the Count! alas, how he is
       chang'd!
His looks are wan and woeful, and he seems
A man that wrestles with ill–boding fancies.
It is not study that has done all this.

BEATRICE: It cannot be, his passion should yet live;
And but of late he has been seen to wear
These knotted brows and that wan melancholy.
Shall we invite him to partake our pleasures?

SIR GONDIBERT: Do, my sweet Beatrice - but see, the
       children
Already press and beckon him to come.

[*Enter* HERMAN, *led by two children.*]

50   BOY: You shall not stay if you will not be merry.

HERMAN: Thou pretty fairy! How his mother's
       beauty
Dawns in his young face, like the budded rose.
Oh, Beatrice – too happy Gondibert!

16

THE STAR OF DESTINY

BEATRICE [*Approaching*]: Come, sit with us, Lord
      Herman, on this bank;
To–day we hold a little revel here
To please our children. See, our rustic neighbours
Are gaily coming; let us view their sports.

[*They sit down; enter dancers, villagers, and* VENTOSE *with them: – a dance.*]

HERMAN [*Rising*]: This sight is hateful to me, and
      the looks
Of these glad cherubs chafe my troubled heart;
Fiend, fiend, where art thou?

[*The* FIEND *appears, muffled in black.*]

–Blast this scene of bliss.

[*Exit* HERMAN *and* FIEND.]

SIR GONDIBERT: Alas! how is that shining spirit
      faded,
The beam and glory of it all eclips'd.

BEATRICE: But come, we must not let this mar our
      sports.

SIR GONDIBERT: Ventose, you dance?

VENTOSE: I did, Sir Gondibert;
But that was when the bouncing blood of youth
Leapt from my heart, and prompted up my heel:
I was accounted then a gracious dancer.

SIR GONDIBERT: Indeed, Ventose! Thou wilt yet try
    thy skill?

BEATRICE: I pray thee do – thou art not yet too old.

70   VENTOSE: Ah, lady fair! to such a fond entreaty,
It were most stern not to be found consenting.
Bid, then, these capering bumpkins stand apart,
And while the sweet musicians ply their sticks,
I will essay to ape my wonted graces.

[VENTOSE *dances – the children and others laugh – in an
instant a shriek is heard – all fly – a wild boar crosses the
stage, and returns, dragging* VENTOSE.]

Scene IV – A Chamber

HERMAN [*Alone*]: The loss of Beatrice was as
    perdition;
And raging passion, like the blasts of hell,
Then swept me to despair – Oh, Beatrice,
For thee a dreadful forfeit I have made,
And yet I have thee not – But I may have.

18

THE STAR OF DESTINY

It is a vantage destiny must yield,
Though I have gained it at a fatal price.
Come, thou dread demon, that art bound to serve me,
Come and fulfil thy part, accursed fiend!

[*The* DEMON *appears.*]

I would have Beatrice within my castle
A willing guest – Go, find the means to send her,
And let me see how thou perform'st the task.

[*The* DEMON *vanishes – thunder – the walls of the chamber
open, and show an old man on a bed of sickness, surrounded
by attendants – he delivers papers to* LUDOLPH; *the fiend is
seen approaching behind, and, in a moment, when the patient
appears to pray, he strikes him dead with a dart.*]

HERMAN: What means this visionary scene of death,
I see there but a pale and dying man
Delivering his last testaments? The fiend!
Ha! 'tis the demon strikes the mortal blow.

[*The vision vanishes – thunder – the chamber appears as be-
fore.*]

[*Enter* RUGENSTEIN.]

RUGENSTEIN: My Lord, my Lord!

THE STAR OF DESTINY

HERMAN: How now, what sends thee here?

RUGENSTEIN: An estafette has come from
    Flaughtenburgh
20   To say your uncle, at the point of death,
Entreats you earnestly to hasten to him.

HERMAN: I am too late – the old man is no more.

RUGENSTEIN: How know you that, my Lord? Behold
    another!

[*Enter* LUDOLPH, *with papers.*]

LUDOLPH: Health and long life to you, most noble
    Herman,
And wisdom to enjoy your prosp'rous fortunes;
I bring you tidings that will please and sadden.
Your princely uncle, the Lord Palatine,
Is dead, and left you heir to all his treasures.

HERMAN: He was a good man, whose infirmities
30   Made smooth his transit from this scene of care.

LUDOLPH: He lov'd you well, my Lord; oh! his last
    prayers
Were for your honour here, and bliss hereafter.

THE STAR OF DESTINY

HERMAN: The fiend did strike him as he pray'd for
        me?
Lost, lost, for ever lost!

LUDOLPH: My gracious master!

HERMAN: He gave thee papers, tell me what they
        are?

RUGENSTEIN [*apart*]: How knew he this?

LUDOLPH: I have them here, my Lord.

[HERMAN *waves to* RUGENSTEIN *to leave the room, and he
retires.*]

)

The bonds and vouchers of old heavy debts,
Due by the father of Sir Gondibert.

HERMAN: Ha! give them to me – let me look at them.

[LUDOLPH *gives the bonds, and* HERMAN *glances hastily
over them;* LUDOLPH *continues speaking.*]

LUDOLPH: The dying Palatine did strongly charge
        me,
To beg you, as his solemn last request,
Never to claim the payment of these bonds.
The debtor was his early chosen friend,

21

And he had long ago cancelled the debt;
But knowing how you lov'd Sir Gondibert,
He thought it would delight your gen'rous nature,
To make this sacrifice to youthful friendship.

50 HERMAN: All the estate Sir Gondibert possesses,
Will not sufice to satisfy these bonds.

LUDOLPH: Nor twice as much, twice told.

HERMAN: Then he is ruin'd!

LUDOLPH: He would, my Lord, were they in other
    hands.

HERMAN: The man is in my power?

LUDOLPH: He is, my Lord;
But being so, you have a noble part
In the fulfilment of the legacy.

HERMAN: And what is that?

60 LUDOLPH: To give him up the bonds.

HERMAN: Never, never!

LUDOLPH: My Lord, my gracious Lord!

THE STAR OF DESTINY

HERMAN: I'll sooner pardon the eternal fiend
That purchased me, than this effectual debt!

LUDOLPH: The mother of the poor Sir Gondibert –

HERMAN: Poor, didst thou say? He shall be houseless
       to,
I will not spare him, or his famish'd brats,
A blanket rag to serve them, when they beg.

LUDOLPH: My Lord, the Palatine –

HERMAN: Peace to his manes!
I'll have a thousand masses daily said
For his rich legacy.

LUDOLPH: Hear me, my Lord,
The dying Palatine bade me relate,
How in his youth he lov'd, and was rejected –
The lady was the mother of your debtor.

HERMAN: What! of Sir Gondibert, that owes these
       bonds?

LUDOLPH: Ay; and his father, who the debt
       contracted,
The friend that did supplant him in his love.
He was a poor, but a most gallant knight,
And to promote their love and happiness,

23

His princely rival, the good Palatine,
Lent him the money that you would exact.

HERMAN: Can heavenly spirits yet commune with
mine?

[*He seems inclined to tear the bonds.*]

But who will tear that everlasting compact,
By which I have obtained this boon from fate.
Here, take the vouchers! at thy peril, slave,
Remit no means the rigorous law allows,
Till every fraction of the debt be paid!
90   Take them, I say! I will not hear remonstrances!

[*Exit severally.*]

End of Act I.

ACT II

Scene I – The Imperial Court.

[The EMPEROR HENRY, The BIRDER, LUNENBURGH, *and attendants, in preparation for a tournament.*]

EMPEROR [*With a petition in his hand*]: A man beset
      upon all sides with foes
Cannot be good. – Thrice has this Gondibert
Demanded the judicial combat from us,
And now he craves to dare another knight.
Who is this Gondibert?

LUNENBURGH: The son of Hordin.

EMPEROR: What! the Hungarian chief that gain'd
The lady whom the Palatine so lov'd!

LUNENBURGH: The same, your Majesty.

EMPEROR: Know you the man?

THE STAR OF DESTINY

LUNENBURGH: All that I wish. – These tales for
     which he fights
Spring from a story that affects his knighthood,
As deeply as the trick his father play'd.

EMPEROR: Ah! what was that?

LUNENBURGH: He had a noble friend,
Count Herman, nephew to the palatine,
From whose free purse he borrow'd heavy treasures,
And with the fruits and other vile devices,
Entic'd a lady to become his bride,
20   Whose hand was pledg'd to his too gen'rous friend.

EMPEROR: We will not listen more to his request,
His blood hath in it some base sediment
Dulling the brightness of nobility;
We strike the recreant from our list of knights,
And banish him forthwith our court and favour:
Go, see it done! We would the world should learn,
That there are races in the stock of man,
Ordain'd for high and virtuous purposes,
And they are those whose old unstain'd escutcheons,
30   Are ever seen among their country's banners:
Come, set ye forward to the tournament.

[*Exeunt the court, &c.*]

THE STAR OF DESTINY

Scene II – A Spacious Alpine Landscape.

[*A stupendous mountain in the distant scene. – The gate of* HERMAN'S *castle on the one side.*]

[LUDOLPH *and* BEATRICE.]

LUDOLPH: Oh, lady, enter not this castle gate!
Here moody misery, and guilt and woe,
Contend for mastership; and here despair
Calls on self-murder with his gleaming knife.

BEATRICE: Alas! I know that your once noble master
Is with a fearful frenzy sore beset,
Else had I not, so poor and woe–begone,
Been here upon this doleful pilgrimage.
Go, tell him that the lady Beatrice,
Implores by all the kindness once he bore her,
That she may, as a mendicant forlorn,
Relate the little story of her griefs.

LUDOLPH: A pity that my heart cannot resist,
Subdues me to obey your hopeless suit.
Enter the portal – Ha! the Count himself,
See where he comes! St. Mary guard thee well!

[*Exit* LUDOLPH.]

[HERMAN *enters, and walks wildly, to and fro, for some time, before noticing* BEATRICE.]

THE STAR OF DESTINY

HERMAN [*apart*]: And richly from her round
    unfolded charms,
Voluptuous Nature, wreathing graces, breath'd
Such taste of warmth into th' embracing air,
That my whole spirit but inhaled delight.
It is herself! Ah, my lov'd Beatrice!
Unsought, unsent for, hast thou come to me?
But, no – no – no – I will not have thee yet,
The means the fiend would use I dare not try,
Yet let me look on that fair face once more;
How is thy beauty faded!

BEATRICE: Oh, my Lord!
But not so chang'd as that far fairer mind,
Whose sad decay hath caus'd that care to come,
Which preys on my pale cheek.

HERMAN: Ah, Beatrice!
How did I love thee once! thou wast my heaven!
And losing thee, I found no middle place,
But down I sunk, down, down, for ever down!

BEATRICE: The heart, my Lord, will yield to no
    constraint,
But you had all from me that mine could give;
The part, weak woman's love, that brooks no bidding,
Was his, that lowly pines beneath your hate.

HERMAN: I do not hate thy husband Gondibert;

28

40   I know his virtues, and could once revere them.

BEATRICE: Oh, then, my Lord, why do you press him
        down?
Why with those cruel bonds that came upon us,
Like troubled ghosts from out the sepulchres,
Do you so haunt our spirits to despair?

HERMAN: Because I love thee, and would have thee
        mine;
Come, Beatrice, come to thy lover's arms!

BEATRICE: Lay not upon me thy unholy hands!

HERMAN: Yet will I clasp thee to my burning breast!

BEATRICE: Help, help! oh, help!

[*Enter* GONDIBERT, *and rescues her.*]

50   HERMAN: Detested Gondibert!
The treacherous demon juggles in his bargain, –
For here she came, free and unask'd, she came,
But only to be ravish'd from my arms!
Hell, hell, where art thou? to my summons straight!

[*The* DEMON *appears.*]

Till thou hast hurl'd yon mountain from its seat,
I'll not believe thou canst give Beatrice!

THE STAR OF DESTINY

[*The* FIEND *quits the stage, and is presently seen, in a gigantic form, dilating gradually as he moves among the hills.*]

The mountain moves, and I dare not repent!

[*The* FIEND *shivers the mountain to pieces – the earthquake throws down part of the castle –* HERMAN *rushes into the wood, and servants come from the gate.*]

> CHORUS: Felt ye the earthquake, heard ye the
>   thunder,
> Peal through the dungeons and depths of the earth;
> Lo, the stern mountains shuddering asunder,
> White rolling waters are bursting to birth.

[*Enter* Ventose.]

> 1ˢᵗ SERVANT: Ventose, Ventose! you that are collage
>   bred,
> Oh, tell us what these prodigies portend!

> VENTOSE: They are themselves the very things they
>   seem;
> See where yon cloud-capt mountain prostrate lies;
> Which of you has the faith to set it up,
> And make it lift its hoary top of snows
> Like a tall Alp again? I am aghast,
> To think that nature, with such lack of reason,

60

70 Should thus, like a non compos bedlamite,[1]
 Turn all things topsy–turvy in a trice.

 2nd SERVANT: They say the earthquakes are when
    devils try
 If yet the pillars of the world be rotten;
 Tugging and shaking them to bring them down.

 VENTOSE: Talk not such stuff to a philosopher!
 Why, know ye not, unletter'd credulous,
 That this firm earth, whereon we stedfast stand,
 Is a celestial orb, and in its sphere
 Doth to the moon perform a lunar part,
80 Bearing a lantern to her as she pays
 Her nightly visitation?

[*Enter* HERMAN.]

 HERMAN: Peace, fool, peace!
 Why stand ye wond'ring at this accident?
 There's not a leaf that falls but brings with it,
 As wide a ruin to a living world,
 As the huge chaos which the earthquake spreads
 Round the proud race of man! and who shall tell,
 Within the viewless beings of that scene,
 There may not be some life as dear to heaven,
90 As the most great and noble of mankind?

---

[1]The Hospital of Bethlehem (Bedlam), an infamous early mental hospital in London. *Non compos mentis* is Latin for not of sound mind.

THE STAR OF DESTINY

VENTOSE [*To servants*]: 'Tis plain he's mad – the
   man call'd me a fool!

[*Exeunt servants.*]

HERMAN: I would possess her undivided heart,
But while her husband lives this cannot be.
He cannot pay – the law gives me his person!
What! art thou there again?

[*The* FIEND *re-appears.*]

Seek Gondibert,
And send him to me, fetter'd, to the castle.

[*Exit* FIEND.]

The Emp'ror has depriv'd him of his trusts,
And may I not in his despair of fortune,
Tempt him to part with her? But I have broken
The slender tie I held in her esteem!
Oh! it is easier in the fiend to shiver
The globe itself into its elements,
Than to constrain the light that beams in her,
To mingle with the fire accurs'd in me!
Did I the Palatine's request fulfil,
It might appease her to forget the insult;
I'll take the bonds and tear them in her presence,
Confess the wrongs, in madness, I have done,

100

32

And so again recover my lost vantage;
Thence, thence, once more find footing for my love!
Ha! who doth whisper to me this device,
Making such thoughts, abhorr'd, spontaneous come,
Like Herod's worms that grew within his blood? –
It is the fiend, with which I am possess'd!
Oh, Beatrice! my guilty love of thee,
Hath wreck'd my everlasting life of life,
Upon the burning shoals of raging hell!

[*Exit* Herman.]

Scene III – The Interior of a Church.

[BENEDICT *and* PRIOR.]

BENEDICT: I found him leaning o'er a splinter fire,
The crimson light struck strong on his dark visage,
And 'neath his gather'd brows of stern abstraction,
His deep–set eyes like embers seem'd to burn,
His garb was faded, e'en the stone he sat on
Accorded with his mien. – It had been once
A flourish'd capital, Corinthian work,
But of the acanthus scarcely aught remain'd,
And all around was grandeur chang'd and fallen: –
See where he comes!

PRIOR: He beckons you towards him.

THE STAR OF DESTINY

[*Enter* HERMAN.]

HERMAN: Leave us, good father.

[*Exit* PRIOR.]

Is the Prior gone?

BENEDICT: He is.

HERMAN: Art thou at leisure to attend me?

BENEDICT: Shall I then enter the confessional?

HERMAN: No, father, for I come not to confess
The sins I have done, but what I would do.
Hungry as hell, love rages in my blood,
And guilt is needful to complete the joys.
You are a priest, a soldier of the church,
And bound as such, by all imagin'd ways,
To spread her glory and exalt her power.
If, by the help of your shrewd casuistry,
The saint I worship will vouchsafe her favour,
All my inheritance I will resign,
Into your hands, for a religious use.

BENEDICT: Hence from this holy roof, thou wretch
accurs'd!

20

THE STAR OF DESTINY

HERMAN: The flash that strikes the single traveller
        dead,
30 Renews the vital spirit of the air;
The storm, that sinks the beggar'd merchant's
        treasures,
Purges the hov'ring vapour of disease;
And all particular ills, bring general good:
Apply the moral, and then think good
Thou may'st do with the riches I will give.

BENEDICT: I'll hear no more. Alas! 'tis ever thus;
The heart that cherishes forbidden passion,
Is apt for every crime. Who, and what art thou?

HERMAN: A wretch abandoned to his evil genius.

BENEDICT: It is not fit that such should roam the
40   earth;
I do arrest thee here for sacrilege.

HERMAN: Presumptuous monk! dar'st thou lay
        hands on me?
Where is thy faithful demon?

[*The* FIEND *appears.*]

Seize that friar! –
Why dost thou pause, and beckon me away?

BENEDICT: To whom, lost man, dost thou address
    thyself?

HERMAN: See'st thou not him?

BENEDICT: There's no one in this place.

HERMAN: Dost thou not see that dark and awful form
50   Standing between us? Look! the earth uncloses,
And he sinks down, having no power o'er thee.

[*The* DEMON *sinks –* HERMAN *rushes off, followed by the monk*][2]

Scene IV – The Castle Seen at a Distance.

[*Enter* GONDIBERT, *with his hands tied behind, attended by officers.*]

GONDIBERT: O he was to me, in my earliest
    kindness,
As my own image in the faithful glass.

---

[2]Galt's note: This incident of the apparition is borrowed from Lord Byron's *Manfred*; his Lordship took it from Pickersgill,(Either the English painter Henry William Pickersgill (1782–1875), his brother Robert, or nephew Frederick Richard, both also painters.) who helped himself to the thought from the scene between Saul and the Witch of En-dor (Samuel 1; 28:3–25).

THE STAR OF DESTINY

When first I saw it there, I thought it him,
And kiss'd it for my playmate. In our youth,
He grew still dearer, even by his faults,
For they were all that in his glorious nature
Made him submit to my companionship, –
Had oracles and martyrs from their shrines,
Told me that ever his ingenuous spirit
Could have endured so base a transmutation,
I had replied to them with blasphemies.
But he is changed, and will not be appeased,
Till he has quench'd his vengeance in my blood.
My fortune blasted, and my honour gone,
To kill me now were merciful; – but come,
Conduct me to the maniac's dread abode.

[*Exeunt.*]

Scene V – A Gallery.

[*A star seen opposite the window at the further end.*]

[*Enter* HERMAN.]

HERMAN: My natal star, whose pure and silv'ry eye
Hath been shut up so long, again uncloses,
Though with a troubled and uncertain light;
It is as if the fiends and angels fought
Between me and the glory of its beams.

Surely some dreadful business now awaits me,
That thus its splendour is so pale and shiver'd. –
My trembling household think me shook with frenzy,
And every deadly weapon have concealed,
10   So work the guardian spirits that would save me;
For now that Gondibert is in my power,
The clotted thoughts of murder thicken in me.
Lo – where he comes; would that I had a knife!

[*The* FIEND *enters, and gives him a dagger from its skeleton hand, and in passing off the stage, turns round its skeleton head.*]

[*Enter* GONDIBERT, *his arms bound.*]

SIR GONDIBERT: Hold – hold! Count Herman, hold
    thy desp'rate hand!
I have no weapon to defend myself.
Though the famed promise of thy youth be withered,
Thou art not yet so fallen from all goodness,
As to destroy me like a foul assassin.

HERMAN: Ah! blood for blood; I have shed mine for
    thine.

SIR GONDIBERT: You speak in riddles that I cannot
20   read,
But if your maniac hatred claims my life,
It must be yours, for I am in your power.

HERMAN: Prepare thyself, thou hast not long to live;
Thy hands are bound, but still thy limbs are free,
And thou may'st kneel to heaven, yet while I strike;
In that – in that thou art the happier man,
For I dare never kneel to heaven more.

SIR GONDIBERT: Alas! mysterious and ill-fated
being! –

HERMAN: Down on thy knees! I give thee leave to
pray.

SIR GONDIBERT [*kneels*]: Not for myself, but for this
guilty man,
To whose eternal woe I thus must die,
I do implore thy mercy to descend.

[HERMAN *several times makes an effort to strike, and the star
contracts its lustre; at last he bursts into tears, flings away the
dagger, falls on the neck of* GONDIBERT, *and the star shines
out with great splendour.*]

End of Act II.

ACT III

Scene I – Chamber.

HERMAN [*Solus*]: Her virtues and his worth have
      conquer'd me;
Yes – in her presence reigns a holiness
Checking the taint of guilt in my desires,
Like that unknown renown'd Egyptian gum,
Whose sovereign quality denied corruption,
And kept the dead in everlasting beauty.
But the dire fiend, that will not speak but do,
Will not forego the bargain he has made,
And I must still be lost – for ever lost!

[*Enter* LUDOLPH.]

10   LUDOLPH: My Lord – He is again wrapt up in gloom,
What if his frenzy should return! My Lord –

HERMAN: Ha! honest Ludolph! Wherefore stand you
      back?
Give me thy hand, old friend. Is thy task done?
Hast thou deliver'd to Sir Gondibert

Those fatal bonds?

LUDOLPH: I have, my Lord.

HERMAN: Thank Heav'n!
But did you see them torn?

LUDOLPH: I gave them to him.

20 HERMAN: Thou hast but half thy duty done, old man:
Again go to him, move not from his presence,
Till thou hast seen them utterly destroy'd,
That hell, which cannot re-create, may never
By spell or conjuration bring them back;
Away, and come not till thou hast done this!

[*Exeunt* LUDOLPH.]

The demon is my slave, and though no more
I claim his power against fair Beatrice,
I may employ him to redeem the wrongs
Which hang like mildew on her husband's fame.
30 Come once again to me, thou dreadful thing! –
It comes not yet. – Has my good angel won?
I dare not trust that hope, but still must call.
Come! I invoke thee by my forfeit soul!

[*The* FIEND *appears, with averted head, and indicating, by
the motion of his hands, reluctance.*]

41

How! dar'st thou question what I may command?
Slave, do thy tasks! I know, when I am thine,
Thou wilt not spare me in thy burning hests!
Go to the Birder's court, and there undo
The wrong thou did'st for me on Gondibert. –
A little space serves for an evil deed!
40   How quick he was to work for me that ill;
But now, when I the mischief would repair –
What, not yet gone? By that eternal doom,
Which makes thy bondmen crave increase of pain,
As blessed spirits after bliss aspire,
I will be answered by thine act in this!

[*The* FIEND *vanishes, and* HERMAN *walks thoughtfully across the stage.*]

[*Enter* SERVANT.]

SERVANT: My lord, my lord!

HERMAN: Why come you on me thus?

SERVANT: The servants of the Holy Inquisition
Demand your presence in St. Leonard's Abbey.

50   HERMAN: I will attend them.

[*Exit* SERVANT.]

42

–One day more – but one,
And I must answer to a dreader summons.

[*Exit* HERMAN.]

Scene II – The Woods.

[*Day–break.*]

[Huntsmen, LUNENBURGH, *and* BERNSTEIN.]

1st HUNTSMAN: Sound the bugle!

2nd HUNTSMAN: The bugle sounds.

3rd HUNTSMAN: Hark! the echo,
The echo replies;

OMNES: And the huntsman,
The huntsman and hounds,
Chide the morning –
O morning arise!

LUNENBURGH: To horse, companions; see, at length
      the dawn,
Blushing behind her curtain in the cloud,
As if asham'd that she had slept so long,
Lets forth her glorious paramour the sun,
To share our sport.

43

BERNSTEIN: Where lies the chace to day?

LUNENBURGH: In the black forest; there a savage
      boar,
Shaggy and grim, like a fierce tyrant rages,
And scares the hinds and honest villagers
From their accustomed pastimes. Not long since,
He burst upon them, and with murd'rous tusks,
20   Snatch'd from the midst a wise and learned man,
A doctor from the University,
By chance, spectator of their harmless pleasure.
The Birder, our brave emperor, hearing this,
Has vow'd with hound and horn to hunt him out.
But we are summoned – all the court are hors'd;
And see, his Majesty himself sets forward.

[*The Court pass to the chase; soon after the boar crosses the
stage, and the hunt begins.*]

Scene III – The Church of St. Leonard's.

[*The Members of the Inquisition assembled.*]
[*The* PRIOR *and* BENEDICT.]

PRIOR: You heard his servant, Rugenstein, confess,
How he foreknew the Palatine was dead;
And when the messenger the tidings brought,
He ask'd, as one all privy to the scene,

THE STAR OF DESTINY

For papers that the old man had bequeathed.
These things are of themselves appalling proof
Of leagues accurst, and damning sorceries.
What shall we then say of those horrors done
Beneath this sacred roof?

BENEDICT: See, he is here.

[HERMAN *brought in.*]

PRIOR: Count Herman!

HERMAN: Well, sir!

PRIOR:Yo u shall answer me –

HERMAN: What have you heard?

PRIOR: Hear us, and then reply.
It has been told, say if the tale be true,
An ancient man, hoary and wild and strange,
Cloth'd in the garb of some untravell'd land,
Came to you in the forest – some believe

He was that wretch who never shall know death –
And nine times offer'd you a magic book,
Lock'd with huge brazen clasps, which you refused,
Till the ninth time; oh, had you *that* withstood!

HERMAN: What might have then ensued?

45

THE STAR OF DESTINY

PRIOR: Within that book
None may without eternal peril read!

HERMAN: Think ye I would confess against myself?

INQUISITION: Hear him no more, but to the rack
      with him!

HERMAN: And so extort the truth! Hold! yet forbear;
30   I know not what your riving wheels may force
From out my torments. – I may then accuse
Even you, my Lord Inquisitor, as one
That shares the guilt and pleasures of my sins.

PRIOR: He is not to be daunted by the rack.
We'll try his faith by a more certain test; –
See, how the earthquake rent our sacred dome. –
Will you rebuild the abbey?

HERMAN: Ha! will that
Be taken as a surety for my soul?
40   If towers on towers, and sculptur'd churches, pil'd
Higher than Babel, would but serve for that! –
As in the earthquake, when the mountain fell,
Your church was shaken, it is meet that I
Should use the means I used, to set it right. –
It shall be done.

THE STAR OF DESTINY

PRIOR: We can desire no more.
My lord, we are content – you may depart.

[*Exeunt all but* BENEDICT *and* HERMAN; BENEDICT *retiring*, HERMAN *calls him back.*]

HERMAN: I would converse with thee, good man,
      alone.
There's a disease philosophy disowns,
In which 'tis said the living frame of man
Begets an actual fire within itself –
And I have caught it – oh! it kindles *here*.
I could not think, till I had felt this pain,
How sweet a boon consenting nature gave
To weary mortals in that sleep of rest,
Beneath the grassy blanket of the grave.

BENEDICT: But to lie down, while yet the pulse beats
      high,
Like an inglorious sluggard in his task,
Bating the sin, is an unmanly part.

HERMAN: Disease and accident, and battle wounds,
Set the soul free while in its noblest vigour,
And wherefore, when it sinks so low as mine,
Should it remain imprison'd in the flesh,
A living being to a carcase chain'd!

BENEDICT: My Lord!

47

THE STAR OF DESTINY

HERMAN: – I think the mind, when it despairs,
Is with a deadly malady oppress'd,
And to relieve it, instinct prompts the hand.

BENEDICT: Oh, know you not my lord where they
must go,
Who do that sin which cannot be repented?

HERMAN: Where'er it is, they take their fate with
them,
And cannot suffer, in another place,
A fiercer hell than burns within them here.
But I have gain'd one deep and dreadful secret,
By the stern quests of my unsocial science.

BENEDICT: Ah! what is it?

HERMAN: When the self-slaughter'd falls,
He but fulfills some compact made before,
With the eternal enemy of man.

BENEDICT: My lord, my lord, what do these words
portend?

HERMAN: Why only, that this being All Soul's Eve,
I would that thou shouldst in thy requiems think
Of forfeit spirits that can hope no more. –
When you at midnight hear –

BENEDICT: What, my dear lord?

HERMAN: Fall on your knees and weep, –

BENEDICT: For whom?

HERMAN: For me.

[*Exeunt* HERMAN *and* BENEDICT.]

Scene IV – The Landscape, and the Gate of HERMAN'S Castle.

[*Enter* EMPEROR, LUNENBURGH, *&c., &c.*]

EMPEROR: It is a vain pursuit, – call in my train.
I'd rather bide the shock of twenty tiltings,
Than such another day's determined chase.
Thrice was the dreadful boar at my spear's point,
And thrice the weapon shiver'd in my grasp,
And he escap'd unhurt! Know you this castle?

LUNENBURGH: It is Count Herman's.

EMPEROR: No; it cannot be!

THE STAR OF DESTINY

LUNENBURGH: It was the Palatine's preferred
    retreat.

10   How changed is all around! See how Neglect
Sits on the rushy margin of the lake,
Spreading her mantling weeds, while Ruin leans,
With ivy tendrils dangling in her hand,
From the lone battlements of yonder tower.

EMPEROR: The place denotes a poor or sullen master;
But be he what he may, here we must roost;
So wind the horn that hangs there at the gate.

[*An attendant winds the horn, and* VENTOSE, *as seneschal,
come out.*]

VENTOSE: What Nimrods are ye, that invade our
    bounds,
Which, save the pretty paw of nimble hare,

20   Or the cleft sandal of the simple fawn,
Nor hoof nor heel impresses.

LUNENBURGH: Ah, Ventose!

VENTOSE: My wise Lord Lunenburgh!

LUNENBURGH: How cam'st thou here?

VENTOSE: Have you not heard of that outrageous
    boar

THE STAR OF DESTINY

That dared with rav'nous throat to seize on me,
And had devour'd, doubtless, but for Count Herman
Who, with a voice tuned to a high command,
Met the grim ravisher, and me rescued?

EMPEROR: Art thou that learned doctor?

VENTOSE: I am he.
And I, in gratitude to brave Count Herman,
Well he deserves the name, have here become
His castle's seneschal, an honour'd office,
Richly endow'd with largess and with fee,
And gay habiliments, behold, to boot. –
Walk in, my Lord.

LUNENBURGH: Go, let your master know
The Emperor will be his guest to–night.

VENTOSE: Ring the alarm bell – let the trumpets
          shout
The Emperor! the Emperor! My Lord,
When will his dreadful majesty be here?
In, in, my Lord; let all your servants aid.
Stop, fellow, stop! my Lord takes precedence.

LUNENBURGH: That is his Majesty.

[*Exeunt all to the castle but* VENTOSE.]

VENTOSE: O mercy, mercy!
Was ever treason, and high treason too,
So guileless done by honest man before?
I shall be hang'd for this, – devoted man!

[*He rushes in despair against* HERMAN, *who is entering, and then flees into the castle.*]

50 HERMAN [*solus*]: The peasants say it is the Emperor.
Fiend, Fiend, attend! – I will brook no delay.

[*The* FIEND *appears.*]

Thou hast done well to send the Emperor here –
Prepare a banquet meet for such a guest.

[*Exit* FIEND.]

The day is far declined, – the setting sun –
Ha! what is that between me and the sun?
A visionary arm whose hand doth hold
A time–glass, and the sands are all run out. –
O! I must hasten, while there is yet time,
To intercede for injured Gondibert.

[*Exit* HERMAN.]

THE STAR OF DESTINY

Scene V – The Banquet Hall.

[*The* EMPEROR, *and all the Dramatis Personae but the* FIEND. *Music, &c. – The music stops, and the* EMPEROR *comes forward with* HERMAN.]

EMPEROR: At your request, most kind and liberal
      host,
He shall in all his honours be replaced.

HERMAN: It is enough; your Majesty so wills it. –
But I had hoped that his own worth and service
Were of themselves sufficient. – Gondibert!
His Majesty is pleased that you again
Return to court: do homage for the boon.

[GONDIBERT *kneels to the* EMPEROR.]

[*Apart*] The ill I did, still lacks in reparation.

EMPEROR: My Lord, upon our eyelids sits dull Sleep,
Pressing them down: again, with thanks, good night!

[*Exeunt all but* GONDIBERT, HERMAN *and* BEATRICE.]

HERMAN: He's gone – they all are gone – stay you,
      my friend!

GONDIBERT: How deeply, Herman, am I still your
      debtor!

53

THE STAR OF DESTINY

BEATRICE: My Lord, my generous friend, what
    moves you thus?

HERMAN: I have done all to heal the harm I did you
Within the compass of my desp'rate means.
Can you forgive me yet?

BEATRICE and GONDIBERT: We do! we do!

GONDIBERT: 'Tis late, dear Herman, let us part
    to–night.

HERMAN: Yes: we must part.

20   BEATRICE: My Lord!

HERMAN: What is the hour?

GONDIBERT: Nearing to midnight.

HERMAN: No, no, – not so late.
I saw but now upon the western hills
The setting sun. As a refulgent spirit,
After a glorious transit o'er the earth,
Moves into Heaven, he parted from my sight;
But mine must, like a pale and falling star,
Be headlong cast, and quench'd in utter darkness.

30   GONDIBERT: Herman! dear Herman!

THE STAR OF DESTINY

HERMAN: O! your hands, your hands!
Time drags me on. – Upon my burning brow
I feel the coming demon's breath of flame.
Air! give me air! O, let me taste once more
That living freshness in the breath of Heaven!

[BEATRICE *throws open a large window at the upper end of the hall.*]

BEATRICE: O look, my Lord, to yonder starry sky;
It is, methinks, the wing of Providence,
All speckled over with bright, wakeful eyes,
Cov'ring and watching all.

HERMAN: Ah, how they speed!
I see but there the restless orbs of time,
Like harbingers of some dread execution,
All marching onward and will not be stay'd.
Why is this universal haste in Nature?
Stand still, stand still! Oh yet, while there is time!
I'll call the fiend to stop their fatal speed.

[*The clock strikes.*]

It is too late. – He comes! he comes! he comes!

[*A cloud overspreads the sky as the clock strikes twelve. – Thunder and lightning. – The* DEMON *is seen in the cloud. –* GONDIBERT *and* BEATRICE *fall on their knees. -* HERMAN *stands fascinated with horror.*]

THE STAR OF DESTINY

GONDIBERT: As we forgave the wrongs he did to us,
O let him be forgiven? As he was wont
To stretch his arm to succour the distress'd,
Let his good angel drive the fiend away,
And from this everlasting peril save him.

[*A stupendous arm appears from a bright cloud, and pushes the* DEMON *down, in the midst of thunder and lightning. – All the* Dramatis Personae *come rushing into the room, the clouds disappear, the star shines out, and a grand chorus sing in the air.*]

CHORUS: A soul is redeem'd, – glad tidings in
        Heaven,
The seraphs' high peans of thankfulness sing;
The seal from the paction of horror is riven;
Shout anthems of glory, and praise to the King!

THE END.

THE GERMAN'S TALE

by
John Galt
(1824)

Transcribed from*The Museum of Foreign Literature and Science*, Volume 6, Number 31 (January to June, 1825), Pp. 47-58. E. Littell, Philadelphia.[1]

The German's Tale
By the Author of *Annals of the Parish*[2]

At the birth of every man, a certain star is appointed to preside, and he who is able to discover the particular orb of his own destiny, may learn, by the changes in its appearance and splendour, whenever his good or evil genius acquires the predominant influence.

---

[1]This is the same version that appeared in 1824 (John Galt 1824. *Rothelan: A Romance of the English Histories; The Quarantine; Or, Tales of the Lazaretto; The German's Tale.* Oliver & Boyd. Pp. 279–314.

[2]Novel by John Galt, published in 1821.

THE GERMAN'S TALE

Few, however, have been able to obtain this important knowledge; but tradition says, that Count Herman of Flaughtenburg,[3] who was nephew to the celebrated Prince Palatine Aadolph[4] in the reign of Henry the Birder,[5] not only possessed it in an eminent degree, but also the secrets of alchymy and magic. The singular things which he was able to perform are the admiration of all the students of the occult sciences; and the history of his own life, as tending to illustrate the peculiar astrology to which I have alluded, as well as to explain in some degree the prodigies ascribed to his faculties in philosophy, is one of the most curious legends in the history of knowledge, and has served as the basis of many wild and wonderful poems and dramas.

In early life the Palatine, his uncle, had been deeply in love with the beautiful Matild, the youngest daughter of Count Albert of Strasburgh; she, however, placed her affections on Rupert of Hemlin, a youth of noble blood, but whose patrimony had been wasted in the Hungarian wars, by which he was rendered entirely dependent on the gen-

---

[3] Most likely Flautenberg.

[4] Adolph of the Rhine (1300–1327) from the house of Wittelsbach was formally Count Palatine of the Rhine in 1319–1327. There is no Count Palatine by the name of Adolph before him.

[5] Apparently Henry the Fowler (876–936), first of the Ottonian Dynasty of German kings and emperors from 919 to 936. "Henry the Birder was the first who introduced Tournaments in Germany...[he] solemnized one in the City of Madelburg upon the first Sunday, after the Feast of the three Kings, in the Year 938..." (*A System of Heraldry Speculative and Practical* by Alexander Nisbet, 1722. J. Mack Euen. Page 7).

erosity of his friend the Palatine. It is commonly said, that Rupert had not acted in the business with all the purity due to his generous patron; on the contrary, that, being employed by the prince as the messenger between him and Matild, he had himself become smitten by her beauty, and used, for his own advantage, that free intercourse to which he was admitted with the lady only on the Palatine's account. But, however this may be, the Palatine, on discovering the mutual passion between Matild and his faithless friend, did every thing to promote their union; and at their marriage he advanced large sums to Rupert, for which he took his bonds.

The perfidy of Rupert, or the disappointment, certainly sank deep into the high chevalier bosom of the Palatine; for he soon after quitted the Birder's court, and retired to the castle of Flaughtenburg, where he spent the remainder of his days sequestered from the world.

In due time Rupert and Matild had a son, whom they named Gondibert, who became the friend of Herman, as his father had been to the Palatine, and, strange to say, treated him, as it is alleged, much in the same manner; for Herman, falling in love with Beatrice of Lunenburg, Gondibert supplanted him in her affections, and they married.

The effect of this on Herman was similar to what the conduct of Rupert and Matild had been on his uncle. He, too, quitted the world, but, instead of retiring to the country, and taking his pastime in the chase, he went to Nuremberg, and, entering himself a member of the college, devoted his days and nights to the study of that strange and mysterious erudition for which he became so greatly renowned.

When he had been about seven years engaged in these solitary studies and occult researches, he happened one afternoon to walk out into the forest on the northern side of the city, and, just at the moment of sunset, he observed a stranger near him. He was somewhat startled by the suddenness of his appearance, for the stranger had come upon him like an instantaneous apparition, and his garb and air were strange and alien. He had a singularly ancient look, and it is supposed by many that he could be no other than the excommunicated Jew, who is doomed to wander over the earth till the day of judgement.

After a solemn and silent salutation, this tremendous person offered to Herman a large old magical volume, curiously bound and ornamented, and locked by seven brazen clasps of the most extraordinary workmanship. Eight times Count Herman refused to accept the mysterious volume. It would have been well for him had he withstood the ninth temptation, but his firmness yielded; and that night, though the sky was cloudless, and every planet and orb of the heavens shone out with unusual brilliancy, the natal star of Herman was not visible.

The instant that he took the book, that strange and ancient man vanished, and the Count returned with it to his chambers in the college. It was observed, by some of the priests in the city and the doctors of the university, under his arm, as he walked homeward; and they were all struck with wonder and curiosity at the sight, for the most learned among them had never seen any volume so richly and so hieroglyphically adorned.

For seven days and nights Count Herman did nothing but study that volume, – and with the window of his apartment open, in order that he might see the star which he had previously ascertained presided over his destiny. As often as he turned a new leaf, the rays of the star were observed to flicker and twinkle with an ominous and fatal intimation, but still he persevered.

On the evening of the seventh day, he had completed his perusal of the volume; and, without speaking to any one, he walked to the church–yard, and gathered certain herbs; he afterwards went to an apothecary, and bought other ingredients; but what use he meant them for the apothecary could not divine. Having thus collected his materials, he procured a large copper vessel,[6] in the centre of which he lighted a fire, and threw in the ingredients which he had previously collected.

By this time it was almost midnight, and his star had contracted its lustre into the smallest possible speck. The Count still seemed to hesitate as he approached a table, on which lay a case of lancets that he had provided, and as often as he paused, reluctant to lift the instruments, the beautiful star brightened its admonitory radiance, and cheered him to desist. But his evil genius in the end prevailed; – stretch-

---

[6]The "*mangaul*" of *The Star of Destiny* (Act I, scene I).

61

ing forth his hand rashly, he took one of the lancets, and, piercing his left arm, allowed three drops of his own blood to mingle with the other ingredients of the caldron.

Scarcely had he with a throbbing heart performed this dreadful incident of sorcery, when a vast, lean, and dreadful hand appeared amidst the smoke and fume of the charm, and presenting him with a roll, on which was written these word: – "If thou wilt yield thy soul to me, unless it can be redeemed by the prayers of those you injure, I will serve thy wishes with the power of a god and the submission of a slave till All-souls' eve."[7]

"Who and what art thou," exclaimed Count Herman, "that dost tempt me with this apocalypse of agency? – Show me thy face, that I may know if thou mayest be trusted."

At that instant a black cloud, which was hovering in the air opposite the window, and which had obscured Count Herman's star of destiny, suddenly opened, and displayed a magnificent being, clothed in light and splendour, and smiling with ineffable and alluring sweetness and beneficence. The Count, ravished with delight at this beautiful revelation, fell on his knees, and declared, that he had no desire to serve any brighter God; but still retaining some of his wonted self-possession, he said – "Show me, however, what thou canst do for me, for I will accept nothing on trust." – In that instant the vision disappeared, the cloud rolled itself

---

[7] In *The Star of Destiny*, this is reduced to: "If thou on All Soul's Eve wilt be but mine, To all thy wishes I will be thy slave" (Act I, scene I).

together, and in a moment after it was moved aside by the wind, and Count Herman saw in another cloud behind it a shadowy procession of slaves bearing loads of treasure, and golden urns, and gems of the richest lustre. – "No," said the Count; "if thou canst give only wealth, I will not accept the conditions of thy offer; for gold can but minister to the sensual wishes of the corporeal being, and my spirit thirsts for higher pleasures."

Scarcely had he uttered these words when a change came over the vision, and he beheld in the cloud a vast landscape delineated as in the scene of a theatre. In the midst of it was a superb city crowned with domes and spires; and presently a great army was seen approaching, in the commander of which he beheld a figure of himself. As it approached the city the gates were thrown open, and a number of venerable senators were seen to come forth, bearing the glittering regalia of an ancient monarchy, which they presented, kneeling at the feet of the phantom-resemblance of the Count.

"No," exclaimed Count Herman; "I am not to be bribed by the toys and baubles of ambition. You would but place me in the sunshine, on a far–seen pinnacle, to make my ruin more impressive than the disasters which befall the common fortunes of mankind. Away, ye empty pageants, ye vain illusions, that the slavish mind alone worships! I have not given my days and nights to the magnanimous spirit of antiquity, to be fooled by such trinkets."

In the same moment the scene again changed, and the picture in the cloud represented a dark forest, partially illu-

63

minated by gleams of lightning, which showed a form like the figure of Sir Gondibert.

"Ha!:" cried the Count, "you would surrender him to my power! No, spirit, no; I am not to be tempted by offering me the indulgence of so mean a passion a malice."

In that instant the view of the forest, and the phantom, and the storm disappeared, and in its stead the beautiful Beatrice was seen in all her charms asleep on a voluptuous couch.

"Canst thou give her?" exclaimed the enraptured Herman, in a fatal moment. "O, let me possess her, and I am thine!"

At these words a dreadful peal of thunder shook the skies; the whole heavens were overwhelmed with tempest and horror; and Count Herman, distracted by the fearful compact he had made, rushed into the open air.

The alarm into which the college was thrown by the sudden storm may easily be conceived; and it would be a vain attempt of me to describe the agitation of the learned professors, flying half-naked in all directions, and the confusion into which many amiable students were thrown by the sudden discovery of the sort of inmates they had taken into their rooms for the night. All these and other particulars it would only be a waste of time to describe; but from that night Count Herman became morose and melancholy. His studies were abandoned, and he gave himself up to the most gloomy and moody abstraction.

THE GERMAN'S TALE

In the mean time, Sir Gondibert and the Lady Beatrice were enjoying every felicity of the married state. Their affection had been blessed with several children, with whom they were annually in the practice of celebrating the return of their wedding-day by a little rural fete, at which all their neighbours, and the peasantry around their residence, were in the practice of attending. On the return of this joyous anniversary, while they were in the midst of their festival, Count Herman was seen to issue from the recesses of a wood, with his arms folded, and countenance knotted with the evidences of fierce and troubled thoughts. Sir Gondibert, on seeing him, was touched with sorrow at his altered appearance, and sent two of the children to invite him to partake of their revels. At first the Count was shocked and agitated, to find himself led thus unaware to witness the happiness of his rival; but the kind and innocent entreaties of the little children won upon his affections, and he allowed them to lead him by the hand to their parents.

For a few minutes the appearance of the gloomy misanthrope damped the general hilarity of the company; but the impression soon wore off, and they resumed their dancing with even more spirit. But their cheerfulness found no responsive sympathy in the breast of Count Herman; on the contrary, it awakened all the worst feelings of his nature, and he hastily quitted his seat between Sir Gondibert and Beatrice, and rushed into the forest, calling for the demon. What passed between them is not known; but scarcely had he disappeared among the trees, when a dreadful wild boar came furiously out of the wood, and carried off one of the dancers, to the total destruction of all the happiness and pleasure of the day.

From that time, as if afraid to trust himself abroad in the world, the Count retired to his paternal castle of Ruggens-burg,[8] where he lived for some time a solitary and wretched life, musing with remorse on the rash act by which he had forfeited his soul without being able to avail himself of the purchase-price. In all that time his natal star was not visible in the heavens; and night after night he walked the lonely battlements of his towers, with his eyes eagerly fixed on the constellation to which it belonged; but it never shone out.

One night, as he was thus contemplating, with a set-tled horror, the countenance of the skies, so totally dark-ened to him, he was heard to exclaim, – "The loss of Beat-rice was perdition to me, and the rage of passion, like the blasts of hell, overwhelmed me with inexpressible despair. O, Beatrice, what a forfeit I have made for thee, and yet I have not courage to demand of the fiend to make thee mine!" and at these words he cried with a shrill and terrible voice, to which all the midnight echoes resounded awfully, as it reverberated among the hills around the castle, "Come, thou accursed demon, and fulfil the purpose for which I am pledged to be thine. I will have Beatrice in my castle a will-ing guest; find the means to bring this to pass."

---

[8]Possibly Roggenburg, Bavaria.

THE GERMAN'S TALE

At these words a dismal and ominous black cloud, like a pall, covered the face of the heavens, and the fiend was seen to approach it, sailing slowly along with dreadful wings. In a moment it stooped, and lifting the blackness like a curtain, exposed behind a stately bedchamber, in which, on a couch, lay the phantom of a venerable old man, seemingly in the last stage of life, presenting a number of papers to one of the numerous attendants who surrounded his couch. Count Herman was struck with astonishment at this visionary scene; for in it he recognised a chamber in the castle of his uncle, the Palatine; and in the person of the invalid, a wasted sickly apparition of that illustrious prince; but before he could inquire what it meant, the fiend suddenly armed himself with a dart, and struck the dying man dead. The whole scene then disappeared, and in the same moment an express arrived in the castle from the Palatine, to inform the Count that he lay at the point of death, and was desirous to see him before he died.

Count Herman, overawed and trembling when he heard this, immediately set out for the residence of the Palatine; but, before he had performed half the journey, he was met by Sir Ludolph, his uncle's secretary, who was coming to inform him that the Palatine was no more.

"Where are the papers that he gave you?" cried the Count abruptly. The attendants, and particularly Ludolph, were surprised at the question; but the latter only bowed, and taking a parcel of papers from his bosom, presented them to the Count.

"There," said he, "are the papers which he gave me to deliver into your hands. They are the bonds and vouchers of heavy debts due by Sir Gondibert on his father's account."

At these words Count Herman snatched them eagerly from the hands of Ludolph, and seemed, as it were, to devour them with his eyes.

The faithful secretary was evidently much moved at this avidity, and said – "Your uncle, my late gracious master, charged me in the most solemn manner to request you never to claim payment of these debts; for the debtor was once his dearest friend, and he would long ago have destroyed the bonds; but knowing how similarly treated you had been by his son, Sir Gondibert, he still preserved them, in order that you might show the greatness of your mind by giving them up even to the man who had injured you, and so, like the Palatine himself, do good for evil."

But to this Count Herman said dryly, – "All that Sir Gondibert possesses is not sufficient to satisfy these words."

"Nor twice as much," replied Ludolph.

"Then he is ruined."

"He must be so, were you, my lord, to insist on payment."

"The man is in my power," exclaimed the Count, with hoarse and horrible exultation. "Go, slave, and at thy peril remit no means the utmost rigour of the law allows, till Sir Gondibert has paid every fraction of this debt."

Sir Ludolph would have remonstrated, but the Count was inexorable, and, in consequence, Sir Gondibert, with his family, was reduced to the extremest distress. By these circumstances, the command which had been given to the fiend was fulfilled, and the Lady Beatrice, in great sorrow, came to the gate of the Count's castle, and sought admission.

While she was standing in conversation with the porter, the Count happened to come out, and seeing who was there, ran and attempted to embrace her; but Sir Gondibert, who had attended her thither, and who at the moment stood concealed behind a tree, on hearing her cries, rushed to her assistance, and rescued her from the arms of the ravisher.

The rage of Count Herman, in being thus disappointed, knew no bounds; he stamped on the earth, and summoning the demon, upbraided it for keeping the word of promise to the ear and breaking it to the sense. "I will not believe," he cried, "that thou canst perform half the bargain, unless you instantly show me that you can move Mount Rosenberg[9] from its seat."

At that moment the fiend grinned hideously at him, and starting at once up into terrible stature, seemed to fill the whole space between the earth and the heavens, and crushed the mountain into sand beneath his heel: in the same moment a tremendous earthquake was felt throughout the country. The Count was horror-struck, and perceived that he was indeed in the power of a mighty and incomprehensible being; nevertheless, his native energy still supported him,

---

[9]Possibly what is now Sulzbach-Rosenberg, a municipality in the Amberg-Sulzbach district of Bavaria.

and he said to the fiend, "I am satisfied; go and bring Sir Gondibert to me." At these words the fiend vanished, and the Count retired into the castle, where, taking his seat at the window of his study, which overlooked the magnificent valley of the Rhine, he leapt upon his hand, and tears of sorrow fell from his eyes, when he beheld the sun setting in all his glory beyond the hills.

In this state he continued for several hours, to all appearance wholly occupied with sorrowful meditations, when suddenly he happened to look up, and was startled to observe his natal star, whose beautiful silver eye had been so long shut, beaming brightly and beneficently upon him. In the same moment, Sir Gondibert opened the door of the apartment; and when the Count looked round to see who was entering, the star contracted its radiance, and seemed again extinguished.

On seeing his victim approach, the Count became agitated by the worst passions, and, in the madness of rage and revenge, exclaimed, "Would that I had a knife!" In the same moment, an awful figure, muffled in a black mantle, glided past him, and stretching forth a skeleton-hand, presented him with a dagger, with which he instantly rushed on Sir Gondibert.

"Hold, Count Herman!" cried the unfortunate knight, "I have no weapon to defend myself. Though the promise and generosity of your youth be blasted, still, oh! surely you are not so fallen from all goodness as to strike me like an assassin?"

"Blood for blood!" was the hoarse and convulsive reply; "I have shed mine for thine."

"I do not understand you, you speak in riddles," said Gondibert, with the self-possession and bravery of a gentleman when in danger. "But if you will take my life, it must be yours, for I am defenceless."

"Prepare yourself then," cried the frantic Count, "you have not long to live. Kneel and implore the mercy of Heaven. In that, Gondibert, you are the happier man, for I must never again kneel in supplication to Heaven."

"What do you mean, Herman? what hideous mystery is in your words?"

"Down on your knees – trouble me no more – I give you leave to pray."

At these words, Sir Gondibert looked compassionately on the demoniac, and, kneeling with reverence, lifted his hands and eyes, and said –

"Not for myself, but for this guilty and miserable man, to whose everlasting sorrow I must thus die, do I implore the mercy of Heaven."

During this short catastrophe, the Count made several efforts to strike his victim with the knife, and as often as he raised or dropped his arm in hesitation, the star contracted or expanded its splendour. At last the better humanity of his nature conquered, and, flinging away the dagger, he fell on the neck of his friend, and wept bitterly; while the beautiful star broke forth with such universal radiance, that the whole

Alpine scene around the castle was brightened as with the dawn of a new day.

In the morning, the domestics in the castle were delighted to find their master in some degree calm, and restored to his ease of mind and gentle manners. Nor could Ludolph believe his delighted eyes, when he saw him conduct Sir Gondibert to the castle gate, where he shook hands with him kindly as he said, "Go and bring her to me – I am now myself again – and we shall taste of happiness; her virtues and yours have conquered." And with these words they parted; but scarcely had Sir Gondibert disappeared from the portal, when the Count suddenly relapsed into his gloomy mood, and hasting back into his chamber, summoned Ludolph.

"Have you those accursed bonds?" he exclaimed the moment the old man entered the room.

Ludolph replied, with a melancholy and beseeching look, in the affirmative.

"Then destroy them, my friend; fly, destroy them; my time draws to an end, and I may be in the interval tempted to some horrible act; fly and destroy the bonds."

Ludolph hastily quitted the apartment; and in the same instant the Count summoned the demon. "Come once again to me, dreadful phantom – wilt thou not come, slave? – for, till my time is run, the bargain was to serve me."

At these words the demon slowly and sullenly appeared.

"Go," cried the Count, "and find me the means to repair the ill and evil I have done."

The demon paused. "Thou shalt go," exclaimed the Count with vengeance; "I command thee by the bargain in which I sold myself."

The demon seemed to glare and gnash its teeth as it reluctantly withdrew. But scarcely had it vanished, when certain officers of the church entered, and seizing the Count as a sorcerer, carried him off to prison; for by this time the rumour was spread far and wide, that he had acquired the mysterious powers of magic, and employed unblest means for the worst of purposes. But the innate greatness of Count Herman's spirit preserved him with a noble bearing, even before the inquisitorial tribunal.

"It has been stated to us, Count," said the Grand Inquisitor to him, "that you have made the dreadful purchase of the book of accursed secrets from the wandering Jew."

To this Count Herman made no reply.

"To the rack with him," cried the indignant inquisitors.

"Hold! keep off!" exclaimed the Count to the officers, as they advanced to drag him to the wheel. "If you torture me, I may, in the distraction of the agony, accuse you, my Lord Inquisitor, of being a party with me in the alleged crime."

The tribunal was astonished at this bold speech, and each looked at the other some time in silence.

"He is not to be daunted by the rack," said the Grand Inquisitor; "we must try him by some other test. Look, Count Herman, the late earthquake has rent and almost ruined this abbey, – will you rebuild it?"

The Count smiled in scorn, and readily promised. He was then told, that he was free to depart; after which, the tribunal was dissolved, and all went away, save only an old and venerable monk, called Benedict, who stopped and looked in compassion on the Count, as he stood with a wild air, for some time apparently unconscious of being observed: at last the Count, seeing the monk surveying him with interest and pity, went towards him, and took him by the hand.

"Holy father," said he, "there is a disease that philosophy cannot explain, in which it is said that a fire kindles of itself within the living frame of man; I have caught it, and it burns here;" and he wildly smote his forehead, adding, "Oh! till I felt this pain, I knew not the virtue of the boon which nature has given. Surely despair is but a deadly malady, and when instinct prompts the self-murderer's hand, it is but the course which the demon takes to work out its natural issue."

"Alas! my lord, these are frightful thoughts. Know you not where they must all go who commit the inexpiable sin?"

"Wherever it may be, they carry their fate with them, and they cannot suffer a fiercer hell than burns within their earthly bosom." In saying these words the Count paused, and taking the monk by the hand, added, "I have learnt a terrible secret by the stern scrutiny of my unsocial studies!"

"What is it?" inquired the friar, with a quick and alarmed accent.

"It is – those who commit suicide, but fulfil a compact which they had previously made with the eternal adversary," replied the Count, with a firm and solemn voice; his eye however was wild, and his cheek pale.

"My lord! my lord!" cried the monk, shuddering, as the Count turned hastily away, and looking back, said –

"Holy father, this is All-souls' eve, and when you hear at midnight" –

"What, my dear lord?"

"You may hear nothing – perhaps thunder, – or the cry of a wretch sinking into the earth. But, holy father, fall on your knees and weep. To pray then would be of no avail."

"Of what do you speak?" cried the monk, almost incapable of utterance.

"Nothing, nothing," replied the Count; "I am an egotist; I think but of myself. Good night."

The Count then left the chapter-house of the abbey, where this scene had taken place, and the old friar stood for some time agitated with fear and sorrow, not well knowing what to make of the perturbation and incoherency of the Count.

In the mean time a stranger had arrived at the Birder's court, and represented to the emperor that a tremendous boar ravaged the skirts of the forest, and that his strength was so appalling that all the boldest dogs and horses in the surrounding country bolted from the chase, and would not approach him. The emperor, being one of the bravest hunters of the time, on hearing this news, forthwith resolved to hunt this terrible boar, and gave immediate orders for the court to attend him by break of day next morning. Accordingly, at that time, with the whole of his nobles and courtiers, the

THE GERMAN'S TALE

Birder took his way to the forest, where they had scarcely winded their horns, when the growl of the boar was heard like the deep lugubrious voice of an earthquake. The dogs instantly fled, cowering under the horses, which, no less terrified, snorted and trembled, and at last bounded away, in spite of the spur and rein of their riders. The emperor was soon left alone; and, finding himself astray in the mazes of the forest, allowed Windfoot, his favourite horse, to carry him as he might, for the terrified animal was not to be controlled.

After riding at full speed for some time, Windfoot stopped panting at the bottom of a precipice, and the emperor, on looking up, saw the walls and towers of Count Herman's castle, and immediately rode round to the gate, which he reached just as the Count returned from the tribunal. The Birder, with his wonted courtesy, saluted him, and, briefly relating the adventure of the day, said that he must, for that night, be his guest. The Count required no explanation of the cause which had brought the emperor to his gate, but, preserving his self-possession, he ordered the warder to summon the household, while he conducted his imperial master to the hall, where he presented Beatrice and Sir Gondibert, whom he found there, with their children, anxiously awaiting the result of his own arrest. Having done this he then retired to his study, and invoked his demon slave again, commended it to provide a suitable banquet for the emperor, and to contrive the means of collecting all the scattered nobles and courtiers in the castle. This

76

was scarcely said, when, in a moment after, the sound of a bugle–horn, like that of the Birder's, was heard echoing in all directions in the woods and valleys around the castle; and presently after the nobles and courtiers, with their jaded dogs and horses, were seen advancing towards the foot of the rock on which the castle stood. Thus, before sunset, was the whole of the imperial court convened within Count Herman's walls; and a banquet was served up, which, even the servants who had prepared it, could not believe was the work of their own hands. His imperial majesty was infinitely delighted; and, at the request of the Count, honoured Sir Gondibert with many graces of his imperial favour before he retired for the night.

During the whole of the banquet Herman was, however, moody and gay in fits; and when the court left the hall, and none remained with him but Sir Gondibert and Beatrice, he seized them wildly by the hands, for it was then almost midnight.

"O hold me, hold me!" he exclaimed. "Time drags me on. Upon my forehead I feel the coming demon's fiery breath. O give me air! Open the windows, and let the living freshness of the breath of Heaven assuage this burning!"

Sir Gondibert and Beatrice were exceedingly distressed at witnessing this new paroxysm, as they deemed it, of his madness; but they led him to the window, which they opened.

"See, my lord," said the Lady Beatrice, as she unclosed the casement, "the beautiful starry sky. It is the wing with which Providence covers the sleeping world, all speckled over with bright eyes that ever watch."

"I see there but the restless orbs of time," replied the Count. "How they hasten onward! They are, methinks, the harbingers of some terrible executioner, that will himself soon appear. Why is this universal haste? – Stand still, ye rash and rushing planets. While there is time I will call the fiend, and bid him stop them, that the doom-hour may never come."

But at that moment the bell was struck; a cloud, like the smoke of a rising conflagration, overspread the firmament, and low and distant thunders, that pealed louder and louder, rattled over the castle. The Count had, at the sound of the bell, dropped the hands of his friends, and, wrapping himself up in his mantle, stood before the open window sublimely awaiting his fate. In the course of a short time, the awful form of the demon was seen dimly in the darkness gradually dilating as it approached. Sir Gondibert and Beatrice fell on their knees, exclaiming to Heaven, "O, as we have pardoned him the wrongs that he did to us, let him be forgiven for what he has done against Providence, and let the arm of his good angel be strengthened to drive away the fiend!"

At these words, a stupendous and glorious arm was seen to issue, as it were, from out the immediate region of the star, and touching the head of the demon, crushed it into the earth. Instantly a shout of all gay birds and creatures of the daylight was heard; and the natal planet of Count Herman was seen like the morning star. From that time he lived a redeemed and happy man; but never did he afterwards enter his study, save only once, and then he destroyed all his books and crucibles, considering the knowledge which they contained only calculated to bring the souls of philosophers into the jeopardy of everlasting perdition.

THE END

ABOUT THE EDITOR

David J. Knight was born in Guelph, Ontario, Canada. He is an alumnus of Guelph and Southampton (UK). He is an internationally published author, with books and articles on Historical Biography, Archaeology and Archaeoacoustics, and was celebrated by the University of Guelph as a Campus Author in 2008 and 2014. Since returning to Guelph, he has written articles for *My Guelph* (2013) and published books with Publication Studio Guelph – *Sound Guelph* and an edition of John Galt's *The Omen* (2013). As the General Editor of Vocamus Editions he has also published *Guelph Versifiers of the 19th Century* (2014).

www.ingramcontent.com/pod-product-compliance
Lightning Source LLC
Chambersburg PA
CBHW032013040426
42448CB00006B/608